Lake Superior

Edmund
Fitzgerald
X
P●20

Ontario,
Canada

P●30

Mackinac Bridge

Beaver
Island P●
14

P●24

Sleeping Bear
National
Lakeshore

P●18

45°N

P●16

22

Lake
Huron

P●26

P●12

Lake Michigan

P●8

P●10

WI
IL

P●6

IA

Ontario,
Canada

28
P●

IN OH

Lake Erie

Published by
Harambee Press

P.O. Box 353
Macatawa, MI 49423
www.harambeepress.com

Library of Congress Control Number: 200593154

Glupker, Dianne/Delsi, Dawna
     Great Lights of Michigan/Dianne Glupker/Dawna Delsi
     Illustrated by Dawna Delsi
     p.   cm.
     Summary: A selected depiction of thirteen Michigan lighthouses.
     Descriptions include: history, location, architectural design.

1. Education/Travel   2. Michigan lighthouses-Juvenile Non-Fiction

ISBN: 0-9769846-0-1
          The text of this book is set in 14 point Chalkboard.
          Illustrations are watercolor paintings reproduced in full color.
                    Covers by DZ'ign Art
                    Text edited by Kristina Wright

Printed in the United States

Great Lights of Michigan

Written by
Dianne Glupker and Dawna Delsi

Watercolors by Dawna Delsi

A portion of the proceeds from Great Lights of Michigan
donated to projects dedicated to preserving lighthouses for future generations.

Dawna Delsi and Dianne Glupker
are both former elementary and middle school teachers.
They live in Holland, Michigan.

Dedicated to our mothers, Helen and Trudy –
two beautiful women born in the great state of Michigan.

What Are Lighthouses and Why Do We Have Them?

Lighthouses are **navigational aids** or shore lights.

They are sometimes called towers or lights.

These lights help boats and ships find their way at night or in the fog.

They help captains and crews avoid dangerous **obstacles**.

Did You Know?

The earliest **maritime** peoples built fires

on hillsides to bring their sailors safely home.

Michigan Has Lighthouses with Catwalks

The Grand Haven South Pier Light has two towers.

The outer tower is a square structure built in 1875.

The inner tower is cone-shaped. It was built in 1905.

The two towers are connected by a **catwalk** that is 1,151 feet in length.

The catwalk was installed to allow safe access to the towers during storms.

Did You Know?

The original **Fresnel lens** of the South Pier Light

was given to the Tri-City Museum in Grand Haven.

It was replaced by a plastic lens.

Michigan Has Square Lighthouses

The Holland Harbor Lighthouse is fondly called "Big Red" by the many

visitors to Lake Michigan and the residents near Holland State Park.

Big Red was built with twin **gables** that show the Dutch influence of Holland's residents.

The Holland Harbor Lighthouse was originally built in 1872.

Did You Know?

The Holland Harbor Lighthouse was originally painted white.

It was repainted red by the United States Coast Guard in 1956

because of a sailing rule, **"Red-Right Return."**

Michigan Has Round Lighthouses

Round lighthouses, such as Little Sable Point near

Silver Lake State Park, are mostly built of brick.

Little Sable Point, built in 1874,

is the oldest brick lighthouse in the Great Lakes.

Did You Know?

Little Sable Point has a "twin sister" tower

near Ludington called Big Sable Point.

Little Sable Point is an exact copy of Big Sable Point

except for the steel plating that covers the brick in the big tower.

Michigan Has Cylindrical Lighthouses

Beaver Island Light, located on Beaver Island, was built in 1851.

It has a 46-foot **cylindrical** tower and a ten-sided lantern room

that offers a scenic view of Lake Michigan.

The yellow brick tower has an attached house

where a former lightkeeper and his wife raised ten children.

Did You Know?

The Beaver Island Light is open to visitors who may climb

the cast-iron spiral staircase up to the lantern deck.

Can you locate Beaver Island on the map?

Michigan Has a National Lakeshore

Another example of a cylindrical lighthouse is the Point Betsie Lighthouse.

It is located on Lake Michigan near the

Sleeping Bear Dunes National Lakeshore.

It has a large two-story house attached to its brick cylindrical tower.

Did You Know?

The large house was necessary because two keepers

and their families used to live there together.

Later it was used as a residence by the United States Coast Guard until 1996.

Michigan Has Pyramidal Lighthouses

The Charlevoix South Pier Light is on northern Lake Michigan.

The tower is open at the bottom with a pyramid-shaped steel top.

This tower was originally built of wood in 1885.

The Charlevoix **channel** is a popular sailing **destination**.

Did You Know?

You can travel to Beaver Island from Charlevoix by either airplane or car ferry.

Charlevoix is 32 miles northwest of Beaver Island.

18

Michigan Has Skeletal Lighthouses

The Whitefish Point Lighthouse, built in 1847, was the first light on Lake Superior.

It has an eighty-foot tower that is supported by a **skeletal** steel framework.

This lighthouse is near the town of Paradise in Michigan's Upper Peninsula.

It has aided ships for over 150 years.

Did You Know?

Not all ships have made it safely to Whitefish Point.

Whitefish Bay is known as the "Graveyard of the Great Lakes."

A famous ship sank offshore in November of 1975. All 29 crew members died.

The ship's bell was recovered and is on display in the lighthouse's museum.

Can you name this famous ship?

Michigan Has a "Schoolhouse" Lighthouse

Old Mission Point, built in 1870, is a lighthouse that resembles a schoolhouse.

It is located on Lake Michigan, near Traverse City.

Old Mission Point has a tower that stands 30 feet tall.

It has a simple wood design that is easy to maintain.

Did You Know?

Old Mission Point is located on the 45th parallel or

halfway between the North Pole and the Equator.

Can you locate the 45th parallel?

Michigan Has a "Castle" Lighthouse

A beautiful lighthouse can be found at the tip of Michigan's "mitten" on Lake Huron.

Old Mackinac Point, built in 1892, has a cylindrical, brick tower.

Attached to the keeper's house is another tower that resembles a castle.

Only a **strait** separates Old Mackinac Point from the Upper Peninsula.

Did You Know?

When Michigan's famous bridge opened in 1957,

ships used the lights from this five-mile long bridge for navigational purposes.

Can you name this famous bridge?

Michigan Has Conical Lighthouses

Tawas Point, on Lake Huron, is an example of a **conical** lighthouse.

It is similar to a round light except it tapers upward.

A brick house was connected to the tower.

It was used as a passageway to protect lighthouse keepers from the weather.

Did You Know?

The original Tawas Point Lighthouse was built in 1848.

It was replaced in 1875 because the shifting sands

moved it more than a mile from the lake.

26

Michigan Has a "River" Light

The Detroit River Light, built in 1885, is built on a **shoal** in Lake Erie.

It lights the way for boats and ships

passing to and from the Great Lakes and the Detroit River.

It has a cone-shaped tower built on a concrete and granite **pier**.

Did You Know?

A ship, named Buffalo, rammed into the Detroit River Light in 1997.

The bow of the 635 foot **freighter** was damaged but the light remained intact.

Michigan Has a "Christmas" Light

The Grand Island Harbor Rear Light is a black and white,

conical tower on Lake Superior.

It was constructed in 1914 to replace the original wooden tower built in 1868.

The light stands at the eastern entrance to the town of Christmas.

It is also called the "End of the Road Lighthouse."

Did You Know?

During the holiday season the light is decorated along

with the rest of the town.

Glossary

Bow: the front part of a ship

Catwalk: an elevated walkway

Channel: a body of water joining two larger bodies of water

Conical: shaped like a cone

Cylindrical: shaped like a cylinder

Destination: the place where someone or something is going

Fresnel lens*: a lens that focuses and magnifies the light by a series of glass prisms

Freighter: a ship for carrying freight or goods

Gable: a triangular feature such as that found over a door or window

Maritime: living on or near the sea

Navigational aids: instruments to plot the course of ships

Obstacles: anything that gets in the way

Pier: a wharf or dock

Prism: a piece of glass used for refracting or dispersing light

Residence: a building used as a home

Pyramidal: shaped like a pyramid

Red-Right Return: as ships return to harbor, red is on the right

Refract: the bending of a ray or wave of light

Shoal: shallow place in the water

Skeletal: like a skeleton

Strait: a narrow waterway connecting two larger bodies of water

Did You Know?

*Some lighthouses are still powered by a Fresnel lens. There are seven orders or sizes of Fresnel lenses. The first-order or size is the largest and can be found on seacoast lights. Many of Michigan's lighthouses used a sixth-order lens.